The
Moon
of the
MOLES

The
Moon
of the
MOLES

JEAN CRAIGHEAD GEORGE

Illustrated by Robert Levering

Thomas Y. Crowell Company New York

L.C. Card 79-87154

1   2   3   4   5   6   7   8   9   10

BY THE AUTHOR

The Summer of the Falcon
Gull Number 737
Spring Comes to the Ocean
Hold Zero!
Coyote in Manhattan
The Moon of the Owls
The Moon of the Bears
The Moon of the Salamanders
The Moon of the Chickarees
The Moon of the Fox Pups
The Moon of the Monarch Butterflies
The Moon of the Wild Pigs
The Moon of the Mountain Lions
The Moon of the Deer
The Moon of the Alligators
The Moon of the Gray Wolves
The Moon of the Winter Bird
The Moon of the Moles

A mole sat up in his bedchamber and lifted his long nose from his belly fur. His home lay under a parcel of the Great Plains of North America—an expanse of flat land that sprawls like a belt down the middle of the continent from northern Canada to southern Texas. It stretches from the Rocky Mountains eastward for four hundred miles into the center of Kansas.

The Great Plains is a land of grass and wind. Forests grow only in protected riverbeds. Once a sea of wild grasses, the land is now blocked off in fields of corn and wheat that are rooted in the rich soils, the hallmark of the Great Plains.

Under the full moon of December-January, the last moon of the year, the plants lay at rest. The temperature was cold and the frost was deep in the soil. Unfettered winds wailed across the treeless miles.

The mice, prairie dogs, voles, and ground squirrels that speckled the grass belt in spring and summer were in their earthen beds beneath the frost line. Some were hibernating until spring. Others were snoozing off the December-January rest period, awakening now and then to eat and stretch. The mole, however, was awake and would soon be at work, for he is as busy when the frost is in the ground as he is when the summer sun warms the soil in June.

His tidy chamber was two feet below the surface of the earth in the center of Kansas, near Twin Butte Creek, Logan County. Still groggy from sleep, the mole sniffed the underworld to determine the weather. The frost had come lower during the night. Ice crystals had formed on the roof of his bedchamber. This annoyed him. He shuffled his feet, dug to the bottom of his rootlet bedding, and sniffed again.

No longer scenting ice, the mole set out to hunt for the worms and insect larvae that would be moving downward from the cold top of the earth.

The mole knew nothing of the earth's surface, for he had never been out of the soil. Born in May in the loam of a farm garden a mile away, he had never touched the leaves of the plump carrots that had walled his birthplace or the stalks above the corn roots that he had cut his teeth on. He was a digger, fossorial, and a member of family Talpidae, which lives under the United States from coast to coast, and from southeastern Canada to the Gulf of Mexico. Seven species make up this family in North America, each a little different from the other according to the type of soil it lives in. The mole of Logan County, Kansas, was the species *Scalopus aquaticus*—the common eastern mole, a loam lover.

When the mole was a month old he had left his mother and three sisters and had dug a tunnel under the garden fence into the wheat field. With a bushel of dirt he closed the route back to his family and settled down to the solitary life of the male mole. From that June day until this frosty moon he had excavated four miles of runways, but he had never made a door or an exit to the sky. The top of the earth was not for him. It was not cozy enough. He needed walls and tight low ceilings, where he could live a snuggly secret life.

Upon settling down under the wheat field he had first dug a round chamber beneath rock in the creek bank. This he filled with rootlets and bits of root bark to make his bed. Then he excavated the runways from this central station until he had five major tunnels. One, the Wheat Root Run, tunneled under the field. Another followed the creek to the east. A third went west beneath the bridge and the road that led to the cattle shed and farmhouse. Another branched off and led up the roadside, while the fifth wandered among the cottonwood roots in the creek bottom.

5

The mole ran all of these without seeing. Moles have lived in the ground for so long that their eyes have become functionless. Skin grows over them. The eyes are mere specks on either side of the head, too small to register anything but lightness and darkness. Some moles live all their one to three years of life without ever knowing light.

Lack of sight did not bother the mole. He had inherited from his ancestors other highly developed senses. Smells and textures were perhaps more colorful to him than a sunset to an artist.

So it was with his nose that he had sensed the cold weather this winter morning. While the wind blew and the birds wheeled across the plains in the early sunlight, the mole began his dark day. It would last only five hours. Then his night would fall, also five hours long, making the twenty-four-hour period on the surface equal to two and a half mole days. The mole's wake-sleep cycle was tuned to his needs for food and rest, not to the light and darkness, as are the cycles of the creatures of the surface.

No night or day exists under the ground, but seasons do. As the mole started down his hallway to his tunnels, he could tell it was winter by the roots of

the plants. Most roots do not die like the leaves, but change their activities. The winter-wheat roots that had come down into the mole's tunnel soon after the crops were planted in September were no longer writhing, but were creeping and seeking. They were taking up minerals and water and holding them in

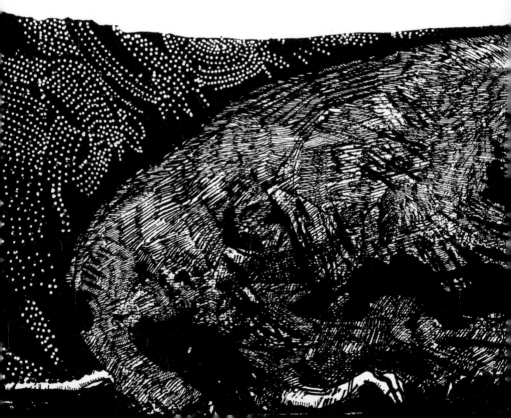

storage cells below the frost line. Some roots were growing at their tips, moving away from the cold. All were stiff and full, collecting food for the growth-burst of leaves in the spring. This fullness of the roots meant winter to the mole.

A root, searching for soil and food, touched his nose. The mole nipped it off and settled back on his haunches to brush his fur. As soft as bird down, his mantle was grayish brown in color and could lie backward, forward, sideways, or straight up as comfortably as a cat's fur lies backward. This trick of the mole's fur was necessary for his subterranean way of life. He could run forward in his tight tunnels, back up, or turn around without being bothered by his fur. It had no wrong way.

The mole did not groom himself long. He left most of his brushing and combing to the walls of his tunnels. Wide-awake now, he left his hall and took off along his Wheat Root Run. Hardly had he gone a hundred feet before he came to a fork. Near it was a shaft to the surface. He had made it when he first dug the run and needed a hole through which he could get rid of his diggings. Pulling loose dirt to the base of the shaft, he had pushed it under his belly and then kicked the dirt with his hind feet, backing up the tube until the soil mounded on the surface of the earth. Other shafts lay along other runways.

Opposite the shaft one of the branches of the fork led to a tunnel a foot or two below the frost line. The mole took the other, a deeper runway, for he sensed that the earthworms would be creeping away from the descending frost this day.

Three feet along his low road he came upon six large worms. They had begun to move downward around two in the morning, when the freeze was deepest. Working fast, they had come through the mole's ceiling and fallen. Now they were trying to dig into his floor. The mole pounced upon them and ate with great relish, for earthworms were his favorite food.

He continued along the tunnel, stepping with his front feet and pushing with his hind feet. These rear feet worked like pistons, straight up and down, for moles have a narrow pelvis. Their little hind legs are free to pump up and down without interference from hips.

This arrangement gave the mole considerable speed, and he moved quickly from worm to worm. He needed about an ounce of food a day—a pro-

10

digious amount, since he only weighed an ounce and a half himself. Four and a half inches long, he was extremely energetic and had a high metabolism. One day without eating, and he would starve to death.

After devouring every worm he came upon in the next half mile of tunnel, he stopped at a boulder. His route ended here, and another mole's property began, the tunnels of a young female who irritated him with her scratchings and squeals. Nevertheless,

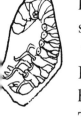

he always paused and listened for her. Today she was not at this end of her runway, and so he turned around by folding his supple spine into a U. He hurried back past his bedchamber and into his Roadside Run.

He ran it for several hours, eating as he went. Presently he came to a patch of loose dirt. Digging, he opened the door to another sleeping chamber. This was an emergency retreat some six inches deeper than the other, and therefore warmer. Packing its root cuttings with his feet, he rolled onto his

haunches and tucked his nose into his belly. Almost instantly he was asleep. The mole's day was done.

Whatever the mole did, he did wholeheartedly. Now he slept with a vengeance. So deeply was he asleep that he did not hear a bulldozer thunder over him and stop at the bridge that crossed Twin Butte Creek. The vibrations from its movement shook his chamber and rattled his bedding, but the mole did not awaken.

Five hours later he got up, straightened his bed, and poked his pointed nose into his tunnel. He

13

sniffed. Air filled his runways. It came from the spaces between the grains of soil, and was slowly changed and renewed. In this mole dawn the earth air was rich with colorful scents. These made images on the mole's mind, through the many nerves in his nose, just as other animal brains create images through nerves in the eyes.

A grub, the larva of a Japanese beetle, was above his head, curled like a shrimp and chewing on the roots of a sunflower. The larva gave off a vivid odor, and the mole could "see" it. He dug right to it and ate, then pruned away a flower root that was growing into his run. The root was vigorous and alive, although its top, the part above the surface, was dead and brown. The mole chewed hard to break off the root.

14

In a quarter of a mile he came to a cluster of buffalo-grass roots that marked the closed entrance to his summer tunnel—a run that lay near the surface, where the worms, grubs, and snails lived in warm weather. These animals would not be in the tunnel in the season of the fat roots, and so he ignored his highroad and worked downward.

Smelling a cluster of worms below his floor, the mole dug toward them like a little machine. His front feet are broader than they are long and are shaped like hands crowned with rakes. Literally they are shovels that dig soil with incredible speed. In one

minute the mole had gone six inches, found thirteen worms, and eaten all of them. Having consumed his ounce of food for the day, he started home to his bedchamber.

He was almost to his main door when the earth spoke to him through his feet. The riverbed was being torn open by the bulldozer. The mole was frightened by the noise. Placing his feet lightly on his floor he listened again, hearing through a circle of hairs on each palm. These sensitive hairs were his ears—the mole has no external ears on his head, just a ring of cartilage buried in his fur. Ears would be a hindrance to a creature that runs tight tunnels, and in the course of time the mole has developed hearing hairs on his feet and short, bare tail.

The sound from the bulldozer shook the earth again, and the mole turned away, ran down his Creek Bank Run, and dug under a cottonwood root.

When his short-lived fear subsided he smelled fur in the ground. Scooping out a quart of earth he kicked it up a nearby shaft, where it lay in a mound under the snow. Digging and excavating, he worked toward the odor.

When the ground gave off a hollow sound he knew

he was coming to a tunnel and he dug more carefully. He did not want to surprise a coyote. He carved the wall to paper thinness. He thrust his nose through, then his palms, and "saw" that the tunnel was narrow. This was good news, for such a run could only belong to a pocket gopher or ground squirrel. The coyote made larger burrows.

The mole stepped into the runway and sniffed. The tunnel belonged to a female thirteen-lined ground squirrel and was sweet with the smell of worms working their way downward. They were feeding on leaf bits and grass blades brought into the gallery by the chipmunk-like squirrel of the plains.

She was in her chamber fast asleep at the end of the winding tunnel. The mole stole toward her and smelled her in a nest of grasses—thistle heads, sunflowers, clover, wheat, ragweed, bristle grass, and prickly pear. She was curled in a tight ball, her head rolled into her belly fur. The leaves and grasses from the surface of the earth were strange to the mole. He paused to touch them and an image came to him. He "saw" seeds and dry, slender blades.

Suddenly, he turned away—he had heard beetle larvae in the ground squirrel's bedding. She did not awaken as the mole hunted them, for she had been sleeping most of the time since November, awakening now and then to gnaw on her seeds, rearrange her bedding, or exercise in her gallery. She was now in a deep sleep under the moon of December-January.

The mole took advantage of her torpor and hurried through her network of trails, eating the earth-

worms and investigating her 500 feet of diggings. They were winding and drafty with winds from the surface. His five-hour day over, the mole started home, listening to his nails click against the hard-packed soil and to the occasional snip of grubs eating the roots of the prairie apples overhead.

Near the hole he had dug into the ground squirrel's runway, he smelled water, seeping toward the creek bed. The ground squirrel's home was over a layer of gravel, an aquifer that held rain and glacial water in the spaces between each stone. The glacial water had been moving slowly through the gravel for ten thousand years. Held in the stones after the glaciers had melted, this water flowed only a foot a year. It was moving through the gravel bed under the plains toward the Gulf of Mexico. It was the "ground water" that men reach with wells.

The smell of water made the mole thirsty. He dug a hole in the gravel, and when it filled with cool, clear water, he sipped slowly. Refreshed, he shoved himself into his own tunnel, blocked the hole with dirt, and sped down the trail into his main sleeping chamber. Burrowing into his rootlet snippings, he fell asleep.

The mole was awakened about an hour and a half

later by the rumble of the bulldozer. He got up, put his feet on the floor of his tunnel and, feeling the tremors to the west, set out east along his Wheat Root Run.

Coming to the iron fence post he placed a foot against it. It was his weather vane to the surface. The mole felt it shake under the force of the wind. The fence post was cold and rusting with dampness.

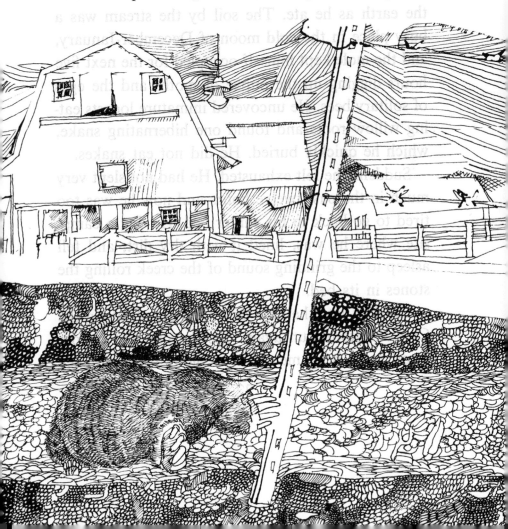

It did not tell him as much about the bulldozer as the walls of his run did. He took his cue from the earth and went under the wheat field away from the sound. Worms were scarce, and he turned around and ran to a favorite winter trail, the Creek Bottom Run.

Near the water he found the snails abundant and dined on a few of these, listening to the creatures of the earth as he ate. The soil by the stream was a busy place in the cold moon of December-January, and the mole kept himself occupied for the next five hours digging up the pupae of moths and the eggs of solitary bees. He uncovered immature locusts eating willow roots and found one hibernating snake, which he quickly buried. He did not eat snakes.

Suddenly he felt exhausted. He had not slept very much in the past twelve hours and now he was too tired to go back to his winter bed. He dug a camp-site where he was, lined it with dry dirt, and fell asleep to the grinding sound of the creek rolling the stones in its bed.

He slept late the next day, then set off along the Creek Bottom Run again. Just beyond the cotton-wood roots he came upon a colony of ants. They

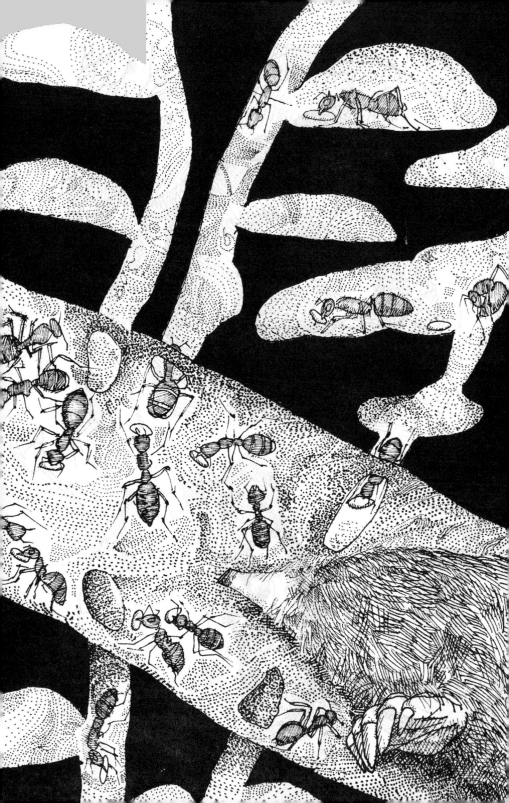

were crossing his corridor as they carried their larvae from the ground above to their deepest nursery beneath a boulder. The descending frost was driving them farther into the ground. The mole ate a few, then began a new tunnel at the end of his Creek Bottom Run.

For the next two days the mole did not hear the bulldozer at the bridge. He relaxed, ran all his tunnels again, slept well, and ate heartily. He could not know that it was night on the surface and that the men who were cutting the earth were asleep.

On one of these peaceful mole mornings he was in his new Creek Bottom Run when he smelled strawberry roots. They have such a strong odor that they scent the earth. In this way they "stake" out territory for themselves. Other plant roots turn away from their chemicals and leave the ground to these aggressive plants. The mole felt a rootlet that had poked through his roof. With a nip he trimmed it behind its growing tip, where hundreds of little hairs

were clustered. These were the mouths of the roots. They took in water and some of the minerals dissolved in it. When the tip grew on beyond the hairs, they would vanish and new hairs would emerge around the new tip.

The strawberry root was a warning to the mole. Its activity meant that the freeze was deepening and that his food would be moving downward too. He made a U-turn and hurried to a musty layer of earth. It was made up of plant life that had once grown by the creek. As the vegetation decomposed, it gave

26

off heat. The mole dug into this warm layer of peat and smelled for worms. He detected them in abundance at the very bottom of the layer, and he dug himself a Peat Run. In less than five hours he was full. Waddling sleepily, he crawled into his camp bed in the Peat Run.

The next day the mole broke into the winter home of a bullfrog. The amphibian was hibernating—his front feet pulled up under his chin, his back feet tucked under his belly. The frog's eyes were open, for he had no lids to close. A thin, transparent membrane protected them from the dirt and grit. The

mole covered the beast, and digging around him, shoveled down to the earthworms.

That night he slept in his Peat Run campsite again, falling asleep to the crackle of box-elder roots that braced the trunk of the tree as it bent in the lashing wind.

The mole was awakened during the night by the smell of a turtle. The reptile was seeking the warmth of the peat, scratching as he moved away from the frost. The mole did not like to be disturbed in his sleep and when his dawn arrived he was irritable again. He bit off seven rootlets of the buffalo grass and groomed his fur vigorously. When he felt better he ran up to the Creek Bank Run.

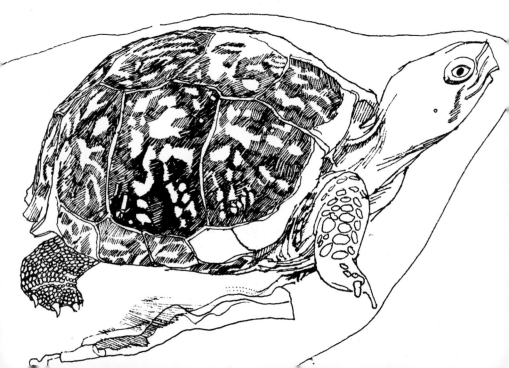

Finding only a few worms in the tunnel he dug recklessly toward a gathering of grubs, broke into the den of a pocket gopher, and stopped. The gopher was awake and shifting his food from one pantry to another. He heard the mole enter and scurried to meet him, screaming and scolding. The mole turned, dug into the floor, and flipped dirt on himself to hide. The gopher screamed louder. Knowing that the mole would do him no harm, he backed to an intersection in his tunnel where it was roomy enough to turn around. The gopher went back to his work.

The mole lay still until he heard the gopher go down a far gallery. Then he uncovered himself and prowled the tunnel for worms.

29

After he had eaten enough he returned to his hole, repaired the break in the wall, and took off for a mile jaunt in his Wheat Root Run. Again the earth rumbled. The mole hunted as far from the sound as he could.

The next day he began another tunnel that would lead away from the bulldozers. As he backed up a shaft he paused. The ground at the surface reeked with the scent of a coyote. Before the mole could collect his wits, the hungry predator had clawed into the soft dirt in the shaft and was snapping viciously.

This terrified the mole and he spewed his musty protective scent, dove into his new excavation, and sat still. His musk usually turned coyotes away, for it was acrid and hurt their noses. This morning, however, the scent did no good. It was December-January; the gophers and ground squirrels were all underground; and the coyote was desperately hungry. He

E. S. E. A.
Title II
Phase One

dug into the soft excavation, and the mole's tunnel fell in.

The mole was cut off from his runs. He would not live long without them to provide food for his ferocious hunger.

Digging faster than the coyote the mole went down into the ground, burrowed west, and came to his Wheat Root Run. He sped to his main bedchamber and threw himself among his rootlets. He was safe.

The next day the earth was quiet and the mole took this opportunity to hunt the Creek Bank Run. Worms had gathered all through the tunnel, and he was so busy feasting that he did not sense a draft of cold air. Rounding a corner he dashed out onto the surface of the earth. His tunnel had been cut open by the bulldozer as it dug a swath across Kansas that would someday be a super highway.

The mole was terrified. No walls hugged him, no soil gave him a sense of direction. The air was loose and vast. He felt blindly for the rocks he had come over but could not recognize them in this strange environment. Clinging to a stone that seemed to smell of himself, he climbed it and came upon the huge wheel of the bulldozer.

The smell of steel and grease burned his nose. He lifted his head. The smell went so high he could not sense its end. He huddled against a small part of the machine. With one side of him touching something firm, he calmed down.

The noises and odors of the earth's surface penetrated his senses. Animal scents blew toward him from the creek bed. The musky mink was fishing Twin Butte Creek. A mule deer had bedded down in the cottonwoods. The badger was digging for gophers. From every direction came the smell of birds: pheasants in the wheat field, crows in the willows, juncos in the windbreak of box-elder trees.

34

The mole had had enough of the surface smells. He tried to feel his way home. As he turned around an astonishing sensation came to him. His head glowed. Sparks crackled in his brain as the rays of the full moon of December-January touched the feeble nerves of his eyes. For the first time in his life he saw light. He was bewildered.

For a long time he sat still. When he became accustomed to the sensation of light he stumbled forward, head lifted, turned toward the moon. He moved slowly. Presently he picked up a familiar smell—the odor of roots and sweet earth. It led him like a magnet to his hole. He dashed in. Closing the exit with a bushel of dirt, he ran in his tunnel under the earth-scar that was becoming a highway—not only for men, but for animals.

Already the coyotes, mice, and gophers—creatures that loved grasslands—were moving east along the new road. The grassy sides of highways provide the food and shelter that certain prairie animals need. They make their homes along the highways. When they have children, the children move away and build homes eastward along the highway edges. Bridges take them over rivers and ravines, and in this way coyotes, mice, and other animals migrate to new eastern territories.

But the mole would not migrate, though his sons and daughters might. When they grew up and left home some would tunnel into the loam along the sides of the highway, and their young in turn would leave home and plow on toward the east, and their young and their young.

37

The mole had traveled far enough. He had left the farm garden and dug to the road, the frontier for generations of moles to come. Now, after closing his door, he dropped his head and rested against the earth, from which evolved all the changing and beautiful animals that dwell under the thirteen moons.

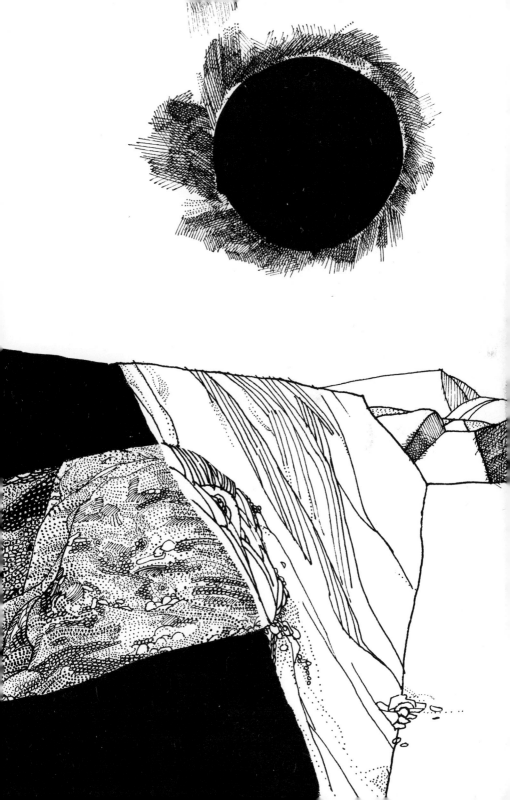

ABOUT THE AUTHOR

The Thirteen Moons series has grown out of Jean Craighead George's lifelong enthusiasm for the natural world. These books reflect her special interest in ecology—particularly in phenology, the study of the relationship between climate and periodic biological events.

Mrs. George is co-author of *Dipper of Copper Creek,* which received the Aurianne Award for the most outstanding animal story published in 1957. *My Side of the Mountain, The Summer of the Falcon, Gull Number 737, Spring Comes to the Ocean, Coyote in Manhattan,* and the books in The Thirteen Moons series all have affirmed her remarkable sensitivity both to nature and to young people.

Mrs. George is a regular contributor of nature stories to *Reader's Digest.* She has held the position of art editor for *Pageant* magazine and served as a newspaper reporter for the *Washington Post* and International News Service.

ABOUT THE ILLUSTRATOR

As a teen-ager, Robert Levering operated an amateur radio station, studied the classical guitar, played the trumpet and Conga drums, and tried a variety of strenuous summer jobs. Art, however, was always his first love. Today his paintings are exhibited in Washington, D.C., and New York City, and his commercial art receives repeated recognition from the Society of Illustrators, the Art Directors Club of New Jersey, the Society of Publication Designers, and the Art Directors Club of New York.

A native of Ypsilanti, Michigan, Mr. Levering received an A.B. degree from the University of Arizona and studied at several art schools in the Midwest and the East. His travels, for both work and pleasure, have taken him to North Africa, Europe, parts of South America, Mexico, and the Middle East. He lives in New York City.